CHRISTMAS JOKES

Gigglers

CHRISTMAS JOKES

Toby Reynolds

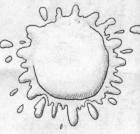

Illustrated by
Andrew Pinder

SCHOLASTIC

Scholastic Children's Books
Euston House, 24 Eversholt Street
London NW1 1DB

A division of Scholastic Ltd
London ~ New York ~ Toronto ~ Sydney ~ Auckland
Mexico City ~ New Delhi ~ Hong Kong

First published in the UK by Scholastic Ltd, 2015

Text by Toby Reynolds
Illustrations by Andrew Pinder

ISBN 978 1407 15655 2

Printed and bound by CPI Group (UK) Ltd, Croydon, CR0 4YY

2 4 6 8 10 9 7 5 3 1

Contents

Silly Santa

Q. What nationality is Santa Claus?
A. North Pole-ish!

Q. What goes 'oh oh oh'?
A. Santa walking backwards!

Q. Why does Santa Claus go down chimneys at Christmas?
A. Because they soot him!

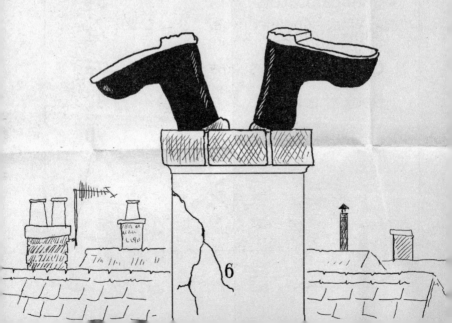

Q. Who delivers presents to baby sharks at Christmas?
A. Santa Jaws!

Q. What goes 'ho-ho whoosh, ho-ho whoosh'?
A. Santa caught in a revolving door!

Q. Why did Santa tie bells to his suit?
A. Because he liked bell-y laughs!

Q. What happened when Santa lost his underpants?
A. He was called Saint Knickerless!

Q. What's red and white and goes up and down?
A. Santa stuck in a lift!

Q. What do you call Santa when he stops moving?
A. Santa Pause!

Q. Why is Santa so good at karate?
A. Because he has a black belt!

Q. What did Mrs Claus say to Santa when she looked out the window?
A. Looks like rain, dear!

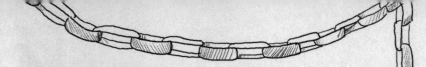

Q. What is red and white and gives presents to gazelles?
A. Santelope!

Q. Why was Santa looking for a new job?
A. He got the sack!

Q. What is Santa's favourite American state?
A. Idaho-ho-ho!

Q. What's fat and jolly and has eight wheels?
A. Santa on roller skates!

9

Q. What's as tall as Santa and as fat as Santa, but doesn't weigh a thing?
A. His shadow!

Q. Why didn't Santa get wet when he lost his umbrella?
A. It wasn't raining!

Q. Why does Santa have a house at the North Pole?
A. Because he's too big to squeeze into an igloo!

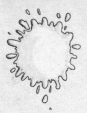

Q. What do you call a fear of being trapped in a chimney with a fat man?
A. Santa Claustrophobia!

Q. Why did Santa think it would be easy to use a computer?
A. Because the elf said, 'First YULE LOG on'!

Q. What goes 'ho ho ho thump'?
A. Santa laughing his head off!

Q. Why does Santa wear red trousers?
A. His blue ones are in the wash!

Q. Why does Santa wear red braces?
A. To keep his trousers up!

Q. How much did Santa pay for his sleigh?
A. Nothing. It was on the house!

Q. Who delivers Christmas presents to pets?
A. Santa Paws, of course!

Q. What do you call an alien Santa Claus flying through the solar system?
A. A U. F. Ho ho ho!

Q. Where does Santa go when he's sick?
A. To the elf centre!

Q. How do we know Santa is a good racing car driver?
A. He's always in Pole position!

Q. Where does Santa stay when he's on holiday?
A. At a ho-ho-ho-tel!

Q. Why doesn't Santa get claustrophobic when he climbs down chimneys?
A. Because he's had a flue jab!

Q. What is red and white and green all over?
A. An airsick Santa Claus!

14

Santa's Little Helpers

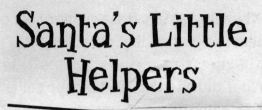

Q. What do Santa's little helpers learn at school?
A. The elf-abet!

Q. What's the difference between the Christmas alphabet and the ordinary alphabet?
A. The Christmas alphabet has no-el!

Q. What do Santa's helpers do after school?
A. Their gnome work!

Q. Why was Santa's little helper sad?
A. Because he had low elf-esteem!

Q. What did the English teacher call Santa's helpers?
A. Subordinate clauses!

Q. Which elf was the best singer?
A. Elfis Presley!

Q. Why did the elf push his bed into the fireplace?
A. Because he wanted to sleep like a log!

Q. What is green and white and red all over?
A. A sunburnt elf!

Q. Did you hear about the author elf?
A. She only wrote short stories!

Q. Why did the elf take his computer to the hospital?
A. Because Santa said it had a virus!

Q. What do elves make sandwiches from?
A. Shortbread!

Q. What do you call an elf who has just won the lottery?
A. Welfy!

Q. How long should an elf's legs be?
A. Just long enough to reach the ground!

Q. How many elves does it take to change a light bulb?
A. Ten. One to change the light bulb and nine to stand on each other's shoulders!

Q. If there were 11 elves, and another one came along, what would he be?
A. The twelf!

Q. What do you call an elf walking backwards?
A. A fle!

Q. What is a female elf called?
A. A shelf!

Q. Why did Santa tell off one of his elves?
A. Because he was goblin his Christmas dinner!

Q. What do elves write on Christmas cards?
A. Have a fairy happy Christmas!

Q. What type of cars do elves drive?
A. Toy-otas!

Q. Why does Santa owe everything to the elves?
A. Because he is an elf-made man!

Q. Where do elves go to get fit?
A. An elf farm!

Q. Who lives at the North Pole, makes toys and rides around in a pumpkin?
A. Cinder-'elf'-a!

Q. What did Santa say to the smoker in his grotto?
A. Please don't smoke, it's bad for my elf!

Q. What message hangs above an elf's fireplace?
A. There's snow place like home!

THERE'S SNOW PLACE LIKE HOME

Q. What do Santa's helpers use to make Christmas cakes?
A. Elf-raising flour!

Q. What did Santa say to the elf who'd broken his arm in two places?
A. Don't go back to those two places!

Q. Why do elves make good listeners?
A. They are all ears!

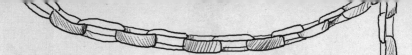

Q. What does an elf do when he can't open a door?
A. He sings to it until he finds the right key!

Q. Who looks after Santa when he's ill?
A. The National Elf Service!

Q. What do elves fear most at Christmas?
A. That Santa will give them the sack!

Ridiculous Reindeer

Q. How does Rudolph know when Christmas is coming?
A. He looks at his calen-deer!

Q. What do the reindeer say when Santa Claus takes the register?
A. Present!

Q. What is the wettest animal?
A. A reindeer!

Q. What's the difference between Santa's reindeer and a knight?
A. One slays the dragon, and the other drags the sleigh!

Q. Who is the cheekiest reindeer?
A. Rude-olph!

Q. Why can't reindeer dance?
A. They have two left feet!

Q. What animal do reindeer avoid at parties?
A. The polar bore!

Q. How many legs does a reindeer have?
A. Six. Two legs at the back and forelegs at the front!

Q. What do you call a reindeer with no eyes?
A. No eye deer!

Q. What do you call a reindeer with three eyes?
A. Reiiindeer!

Q. What's worse than Rudolph with a runny nose?
A. Frosty the Snowman with a hot flush!

Q. What do reindeer have that no other animals have?
A. Baby reindeer!

Q. What sport do reindeer play at home?
A. Stable tennis!

Q. What do reindeer and snowballs have in common?
A. They're both brown, except the snowballs!

Q. What do you call a reindeer in the Sahara desert?
A. Lost!

Q. Why did no one bid for Rudolph and Blitzen at the online auction?
A. They were two deer!

Q. Which reindeer can jump higher than a house?
A. They all can. Houses can't jump!

Q. Why does Santa use reindeer to pull his sleigh?
A. Moose can't fly!

Q. Why do reindeer wear fur coats?
A. Because they look silly in snowsuits!

Elf: I'm so strong I could lift a reindeer with one hand.
Santa: Great, but where are we going to find a one-handed reindeer?

Q. Did Rudolph go to a regular school?
A. No. He was elf-taught!

Q. Why did Rudolph the Red-nosed Reindeer cross the road?
A. To prove he wasn't a chicken!

Q. How do reindeer take photographs?
A. They take elfies with their North Pole-aroid cameras!

Q. What do you call a reindeer wearing ear muffs?
A. Anything you want because he can't hear you!

Q. How do you get into Rudolph's house?
A. You ring the deer bell, of course!

Q. Why did Santa name two of his reindeer Edward?
A. Because two Eds are better than one!

Bonkers
Christmas Books

'HOW TO RIDE A SLEDGE' BY I. C. BOTTOM

'Guessing My Gift' by P. King

'How to Get a Great Present' by B. Good

'Nothing In My Stocking' by Y. Me

'Season's Greetings' by Mary Christmas

'WHAT DID I DO WRONG THIS YEAR?'
BY KOLE N. STOCKING

'It's Cold' by I. M. Freezing

'CHRISTMAS COOKBOOK' BY GINGER BREADMANN

'Singing In The Streets' by Carol Ling

'Disappointing Gifts' by M. T. Box

'Christmas Cooking for Large Families' by Morris Merrier

'MELTED SNOWMAN' BY SONNY DAY

'Christmas Laughs' by Joe Kur

'Christmas Kisses' by Miss L. Toe

'COUNTING CHRISTMAS CARDS' BY ADAM UP

'What To Wear In Winter' by Mahatma Coate

'Where Is Santa?' by Miles A. Way

'Christmas Errors And Accidents'
by Miss Takes and Miss Haps

'101 Cures for Indigestion' by Ivor Pain

'I DROPPED THE CHRISTMAS CAKE' BY S. PLATT

'The Surprise Present' by Omar Gosh

'THE TWELFTH MONTH' BY DEE SEMBER

'Where Is The North Pole?' by Farrah Way

'A Festive Breakfast' by Hammond Deggs

'When Christmas Is Over' by Jan U. Airey

'Sending Christmas Cards' by Bess Twishes

'EVERYONE IS WELCOME AT CHRISTMAS' BY DORIS OPEN

'Stunned Over Christmas' by Holly Daze

Festive Food

Q. How does Good King Wenceslas like his pizzas?
A. Deep pan, crisp and even!

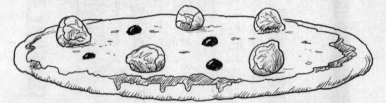

Q. What do vampires put on their turkey at Christmas?
A. Grave-y!

Q. What do ducks do before Christmas dinner?
A. Pull their Christmas quackers!

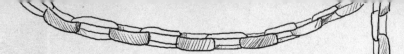

Q. Who beats his chest and swings from Christmas cake to Christmas cake?
A. Tarzipan!

Q. What's the best thing to put into a Christmas cake?
A. Your teeth!

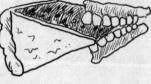

Q. Who is never hungry at Christmas?
A. The turkey. He's always stuffed!

Q. What's the most common wine at Christmas?
A. Do I have to have Brussels sprouts?

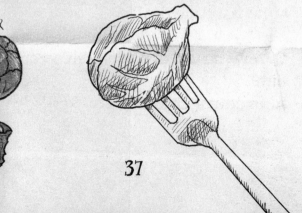

Q. What do you call a secret agent in a Christmas pie factory?
A. A mince spy!

Q. What do ghosts eat for Christmas dinner?
A. Spook-etti!

Q. Why did Grandpa put jelly and sponge in one ear and a glass of sherry in the other?
A. He is a trifle deaf!

Q. What do you drain Brussels sprouts with?
A. An advent colander!

Q. Did you hear about the stupid turkey?
A. It was looking forward to Christmas!

Knock, knock.
Who's there?
Doughnut.
Doughnut who?
Doughnut open until Christmas!

Knock, knock.
Who's there?
Arthur.
Arthur who?
Arthur any mince pies left?

Q. Why did the turkey want to join the band?
A. Because he already had the drumsticks!

Q. Why is a Christmas pudding like the ocean?
A. It's full of currants!

Q. Why did the Christmas cake go to the doctor?
A. It was feeling crummy!

Q. What happened to the sheepdog who ate too much Christmas trifle?
A. He got the Collie-wobbles!

Q. Why did the Christmas turkey taste disgusting?
A. It was a foul roast!

Q. Why wouldn't the teddy bear eat any Christmas cake?
A. He was already stuffed!

Q. What two things should you never eat before breakfast on Christmas Day?
A. Lunch and dinner!

Q. What vegetable eliminates the need to brush your teeth?
A. Bristle sprouts!

Q. What's the difference between Brussels sprouts and snot?
A. Children won't eat Brussels sprouts!

Q. What vegetable can tie your stomach in knots?
A. String beans!

Q. Which beans are never served with Christmas lunch?
A. Jelly beans!

Q. What's the fastest cake in the world?
A. Meriiiiiiiiiiiiiiiinnnnnnnnnnngue!

Q. What did the Christmas turkey say to the unhappy chicken?
A. What's eating you?

Q. What position do turkeys play in the World Series?
A. First baste!

Q. Why did the one-eyed turkey cross the road?
A. To get to the Bird's Eye shop!

Peculiar Presents

Q. How do you know when Santa's in the room?
A. You can sense his presents!

Q. What mobile phone would Santa give you for Christmas?
A. A pay-as-you-ho ho ho!

Ho Ho Ho!

Knock, knock.
Who's there?
Wanda.
Wanda who?
Wanda know what you're getting for Christmas?

Q. Where do sheep buy their Christmas presents?
A. Wool-mart!

Q. How did Mrs Claus feel when she forgot to give her goldfish a present?
A. Gill-ty!

Q. Why don't aliens celebrate Christmas?
A. Because they don't want to give away their presents!

Q. What do you give an artistic dog for Christmas?
A. A fetch-a-sketch!

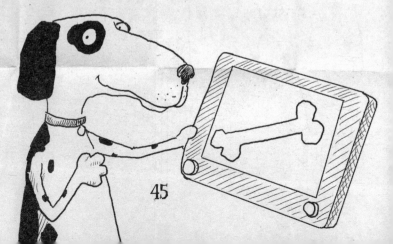

45

Q. What does Sherlock Holmes want for Christmas?
A. Santa Clues!

Child: Mummy, Mummy! Can I have a puppy for Christmas?
Mother: Certainly not! You can have turkey like everyone else.

Q. Why does Rudolph give his friends umbrellas for Christmas?
A. Because he's a rain deer!

Q. What did the octopus want for Christmas?
A. Four pairs of gloves!

Q. What's the worst thing to get for Christmas?
A. Measles!

Q. Where does the Queen do her Christmas shopping?
A. Newcastle!

Q. What would a biker like to see under the Christmas tree?
A. A Holly Davidson!

Q. What did the electrician get for Christmas?
A. Shorts!

Q. What would a gardener like for Christmas?
A. A hoe-hoe-hoe!

Q. What do you get when you cross an archer with a gift-wrapper?
A. Ribbon Hood!

Q. Who would want a Christmas jumper decorated with rabbits?
A. Warren!

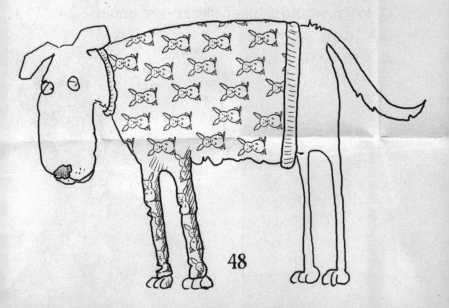

Q. How many presents can Santa fit in an empty sack?
A. Only one, after that it's not empty any more!

Q. What is the best Christmas present in the world?
A. A broken drum – you can't beat it!

Q. How do skunks wrap their presents?
A. They use smell-o-tape!

Q. What do you call a lobster that won't share its Christmas presents?
A. Shell-fish!

Knock, knock.
Who's there?
Rabbit.
Rabbit who?
Rabbit up carefully, it's a present!

Q. Who delivers Christmas presents to elephants?
A. Elephanta Claus!

Q. What happened to the man who shoplifted a calendar at Christmas?
A. He got twelve months!

Q. Which musical instruments did the fisherman want for Christmas?
A. Cast-a-nets!

Q. What did the husband buy his wife after she had asked for something with diamonds?
A. A pack of cards!

Q. What do witches use to wrap their presents?
A. Spell-o-tape!

Q. What did the farmer want for Christmas?
A. A cow-culator!

Q. Why didn't the schoolboy want a pocket calculator for Christmas?
A. He already knew how many pockets he had!

Q. What did the bald man say when he received a comb for Christmas?
A. Thanks, I'll never part with it!

Q. What did the dog get for Christmas?
A. A new mobile bone!

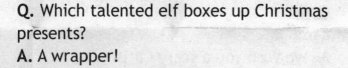

Q. Which talented elf boxes up Christmas presents?
A. A wrapper!

Q. Why do Egyptian mummies like Christmas so much?
A. Because of all the wrapping!

Comical Carols

Q. What is the best carol for a vegetarian?
A. Peas on earth and goodwill to all men!

Q. Why don't computers work over Christmas?
A. Because no creature was stirring, not even a mouse!

Q. What is a ghost's favourite Christmas carol?
A. We wish you a scary Christmas.

Q. When do you drink eggnog?
A. On the thirst day of Christmas!

Q. What is a wolf's favourite carol?
A. Deck the Howls!

Q. What do farmers sing when they go carolling?
A. I'm dreaming of a wheat Christmas!

Q. What do dogs sing at Christmas?
A. Bark, the herald angels sing!

Q. Who sings 'White Christmas' and explodes?
A. Bang Crosby!

Q. What is Mr and Mrs Claus's favourite song?
A. An icicle made for two!

Q. Which carol is sung in laundrettes?
A. When shepherds washed their socks by night!

56

Q. What did the grape say to the raisin?
A. 'Tis the season to be jelly!

Q. Why is Rudolph a weather expert?
A. Because Rudolph the Red knows rain, dear!

Q. What carol did King Arthur sing at the Round Table?
A. Silent Knight!

Q. What did the Inuit sing when he got his Christmas dinner?
A. Whale meat again, don't know where, don't know when!

Q. What is a vampire's favourite Christmas song?
A. I'm dreaming of a bite Christmas!

Q. What carol is heard in the desert?
A. Oh camel ye faithful!

Knock, knock.
Who's there?
Oakham.
Oakham who?
Oakham all ye faithful!

Q. What is a hairdresser's favourite Christmas carol?
A. Oh comb, all ye faithful!

Knock, knock.
Who's there?
Wayne.
Wayne who?
Wayne in a manger.

Q. What do monsters sing at Christmas?
A. Deck the halls with poison ivy, tra la la la la la...

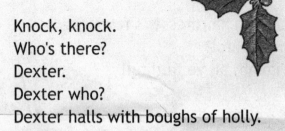

Knock, knock.
Who's there?
Dexter.
Dexter who?
Dexter halls with boughs of holly.

Q. What is a parent's favourite Christmas carol?
A. Silent night!

Q. What do fish sing under the ocean during the winter?
A. Christmas corals!

Q. What's a gorilla's favourite Christmas carol?
A. King Kong Merrily on High!

Knock, knock.
Who's there?
Hanna.
Hanna who?
Hanna partridge in a pear tree!

Q. Which famous British playwright was terrified of Christmas?
A. Noël Coward!

Q. What do monkeys sing at Christmas?
A. Jungle bells, jungle bells!

Q. What is a web master's favourite hymn?
A. Oh, dot com all ye faithful!

Knock, knock.
Who's there?
Holly.
Holly who?
Holly-days are here again!

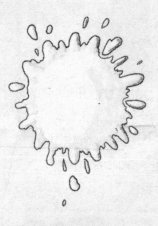

Snow-time!

Q. How much difference is there between the North Pole and the South Pole?
A. All the difference in the world!

Q. Where do snowmen keep their money?
A. In a snow bank!

Q. Why did the snowman love his job?
A. Because there's no business like snow business!

Q. What does a snowman do on his day off?
A. Chill out!

Q. Why does everybody like Frosty the Snowman?
A. Because he is so cool!

Q. What do you call a snowman with a six pack?
A. An abdominal snowman!

Q. What's an ig?
A. A snow house without a loo!

Q. What kind of maths do snowy owls like?
A. Owlgebra!

Q. What do snowmen eat for lunch?
A. Icebergers with chilly sauce!

Q. If you live in an igloo, what's the worst thing about global warming?
A. A lack of privacy!

Q. How do you know if there's a snowman in your bed?
A. You wake up wet!

Q. What do you call an old snowman?
A. Water!

Q. What do you get when you cross a snowman and a vampire?
A. Frostbite!

Q. What did the snowman and his wife put over their baby's crib?
A. A snowmobile!

Q. What do snowmen eat for breakfast?
A. Frosted flakes!

Q. What do snowmen call their offspring?
A. Chill-dren!

Q. What sort of cakes do snowmen like?
A. The ones with thick icing!

Q. What is a snowman's favourite
Mexican food?
A. Brrrr-itos!

Q. What should you sing at a snowman's
birthday party?
A. Freeze a jolly good fellow!

Q. How does a snowman get to work?
A. By icicle!

Q. What often falls at the North Pole but never gets hurt?
A. Snow!

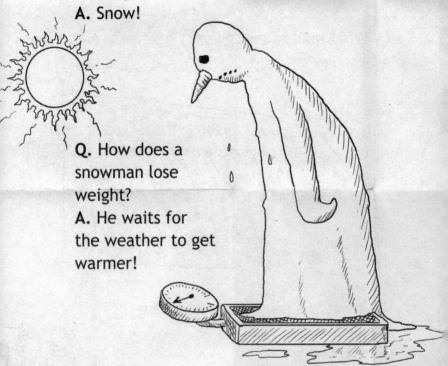

Q. How does a snowman lose weight?
A. He waits for the weather to get warmer!

Q. Where do snowmen go to dance?
A. A snow ball!

Q. What's white and goes up?
A. A confused snowflake!

Q. How do snowmen greet each other?
A. "Ice to meet you!"

Q. What kind of ball doesn't bounce?
A. A snowball!

Q. Why does it sometimes snow at Christmas?
A. Because it's in Decembrrrr!

Q. Who is a snowman's favourite relation?
A. Aunt Arctica!

Q. How do you scare a snowman?
A. Show him a hairdryer!

Q. What happened when the snowman annoyed the snow-woman?
A. She gave him the cold shoulder!

Q. What do you call a snowman in the summer?
A. A puddle!

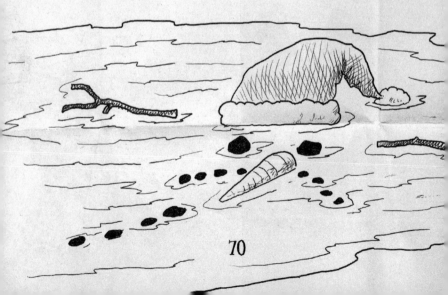

Q. What do snowmen wear on their heads?
A. Ice caps!

Q. What does a snowman take when he gets ill?
A. A chill pill!

Q. When is a boat like a pile of snow?
A. When it's adrift!

71

Q. What does Jack Frost like best about school?
A. Snow and tell!

Q. What do you get if you cross a witch with an iceberg?
A. A cold spell!

Q. How does an Inuit build a house?
A. Igloos it together!

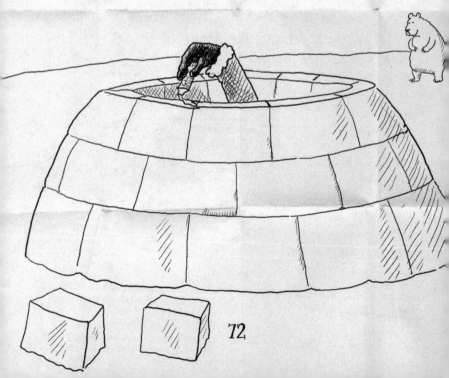

Christmas Trees

Knock, knock.
Who's there?
Tree.
Tree who?
Tree wise men.

Q. Where do rich Christmas trees live?
A. Tinsel Town!

Q. Which sport do Christmas trees like?
A. Al-pine skiing!

Q. What do you call a Christmas tree with a big nose?
A. Pine-occhio!

Q. What kind of tree is always warm?
A. A fir tree!

Q. Why are Christmas trees bad knitters?
A. They drop their needles!

Q. If Christmas trees can't knit, what can they do?
A. Needlepoint, of course!

Q. How do Christmas trees stay fresh?
A. By sucking on orna-mints!

Q. Who checks Christmas tree lights?
A. The elf and safety officer!

Q. What would you have if Santa left a kitten and a puppy under the tree?
A. A meowy Christmas and a yappy New Year!

Q. What do reindeer hang on their Christmas trees?
A. Hornaments!

Q. What did the Christmas tree say to the light bulb when it was sad?
A. Lighten up!

Q. Why are Christmas trees so fond of the past?
A. Because the present's beneath them!

Q. What makes a Christmas tree noisy?
A. Its bark!

Q. How did Noah decorate the Christmas tree on the Ark?
A. With oar-naments!

Q. What's red, white and blue on the Christmas tree?
A. A sad candy cane!

Q. What did one Christmas tree angel say to the other?
A. Halo there!

Q. What is the best place to put your Christmas tree?
A. Between Christmas two and Christmas four!

Q. What do sad Christmas trees do?
A. Pine a lot!

Q. What did the beaver say to the Christmas tree?
A. Nice gnawing you!

Q. What did one Christmas tree say to the other?
A. I've got a present fir you!

Q. How do Christmas trees use the Internet?
A. They log on!

Q. What did the Christmas tree do when the bank closed?
A. It started a new branch!

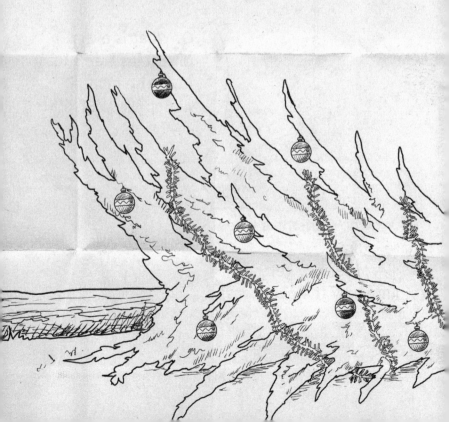

Q. Where do young Christmas trees go to learn?
A. Elementree school!

Q. What is every Christmas tree's least favourite month?
A. SepTIMMMBERRR!

Q. Why do Christmas trees hate exams?
A. Because they get stumped by the questions!

80

Q. What did the Christmas tree wear to the pool party?
A. Swimming trunks!

Q. Why did the Christmas tree go to the doctor?
A. It was feeling a little green!

Q. What did the Christmas tree say to the bauble?
A. Don't you get tired of hanging around?

Deck the Halls

Q. How do you get an elephant into a Christmas cracker?
A. Take the hat out first!

Q. What do sheep write on their Christmas cards?
A. Christmas bleatings!

Q. What do crocodiles play at Christmas parties?
A. Snap!

Q. What game do cows play after Christmas lunch?
A. Moo-sical chairs!

Q. How do fish decorate their aquariums in December?
A. With a Christmas reef!

Q. What comes at the end of Christmas Day?
A. The letter 'Y'!

Q. How long does a Christmas candle burn?
A. For about a wick!

Q. Where does Santa go to learn how to slide down chimneys?
A. A chimnasium!

Q. What's a ghost's favourite Christmas entertainment?
A. A phantomime!

Q. Which Christmas pantomine star is really bad at football?
A. Cinderella. She has a pumpkin for a coach!

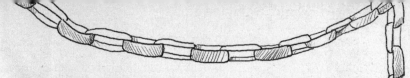

Q. What do you call a can wearing a Christmas hat?
A. A merry can!

Q. What do you get if you cross an iPad with a Christmas tree?
A. A pineapple!

Q. What is green, covered with tinsel and goes 'ribbet ribbet'?
A. A mistle-toad!

Q. Where does mistletoe go to become famous?
A. Holly-wood!

Q. If athletes get athlete's foot, what do rocket scientists get at Christmas?
A. Missile-toe!

Q. What does Dracula write on his Christmas cards?
A. Best vicious of the season!

Q. What do you get when you cross a bell with a skunk?
A. Jingle smells!

Q. What do you get if you cross mistletoe and a duck?
A. A Christmas quacker!

Q. What is the most popular king at Christmas?
A. A stocking!

Q. What has fins, a tail and is posted to you at Christmas?
A. A Christmas cod!

Q. What did one Christmas bell say to the other?
A. Give me a ring sometime!

Q. Where is the cheapest place to buy Christmas decorations?
A. On the winternet!

Q. What did one Christmas stocking say to another?
A. Fancy hanging out at the fireplace tonight?

Q. Why is it hard to find advent calendar?
A. Because their days are numbered!

Q. What do angry mice send at Christmas?
A. Cross-mouse cards!

Q. What happens when you eat Christmas tree decorations?
A. You get tinsel-itis!

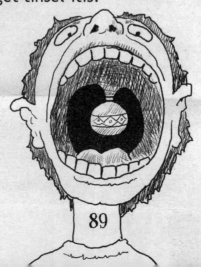

And Finally...

Knock, knock.
Who's there?
Mary.
Mary who?
Mary Christmas!

Also available

PLUS...

SPORTY JOKES

From football and cricket to athletics
and swimming, there are over 300 jokes
for sports fans of every kind!

COMING SOON!